TIME
FOR KIDS

Where Does Your Money Go?

Christine Dugan

Consultants

Timothy Rasinski, Ph.D.
Kent State University

Lori Oczkus
Literacy Consultant

Rich Levitt
Certified Public Accountant

Based on writing from
TIME For Kids. *TIME For Kids* and the *TIME For Kids* logo are registered trademarks of TIME Inc. Used under license.

Publishing Credits
Dona Herweck Rice, *Editor-in-Chief*
Lee Aucoin, *Creative Director*
Jamey Acosta, *Senior Editor*
Lexa Hoang, *Designer*
Stephanie Reid, *Photo Editor*
Shelly Buchanan, *Contributing Author*
Rachelle Cracchiolo, *M.S.Ed., Publisher*

Image Credits: pp.9 (background), 54 (left), 56 (bottom) Alamy; pp.37 (bottom), 50, 57 Associated Press; p.43 Corbis; pp.7, 45 Getty Images; p.8 iStockphoto; p.32 (right) ChinFotoPress/Newscom; pp.23 (top), 36 Newscom; pp.3–4, 9 (bottom), 23 (bottom), 38, 53, 55 (bottom) REUTERS/Newscom; p.23 (middle) ADC-DIFFUSION/SIPA/Newscom; p.52 Los Angeles Daily News/Newscom; pp.22, 28–29 Timothy J. Bradley; p.6 Photo Researchers, Inc.; All other images from Shutterstock.

Teacher Created Materials

5301 Oceanus Drive
Huntington Beach, CA 92649-1030
http://www.tcmpub.com
ISBN 978-1-4333-4909-6
© 2013 Teacher Created Materials, Inc.
Printed in Malaysia
Thumbprints.27317

Table of Contents

Ways We Spend 4

Where Does the Money Go? 24

Making Money Matter 44

Glossary 58

Index 60

Bibliography 62

More to Explore 63

About the Author 64

Ways We Spend

People spend money on everything from silly socks to important medicines. Adults spend money on basic needs such as housing, food, and transportation. They also spend money on extras such as entertainment and vacations. Kids buy treats to eat, games to play, and things to wear. Kids also use money for mini-golf, amusement parks, seeing movies, and other fun activities. How do you spend your money? Where does your money go?

Sources of Income

People are able to shop for things because they have earned money. Most adults earn money from a job. The **income** they earn is paid to them in exchange for their hard work.

Young spenders may not be old enough to work full-time, but that doesn't mean that kids can't have their own money. Kids can earn money from a part-time job, such as babysitting or mowing lawns. Some get an **allowance** by doing chores around the house.

4

THINK LINK

- ✦ How do we spend money?
- ✦ What do we use money to buy?
- ✦ What are other ways we can use money?

There are lots of ways you can earn extra money on the weekend just working around your neighborhood.

Purchasing Power

People use different items when they spend money. Some spenders use cash, which includes bills and coins. Others use **checks** or **debit cards**. These take money directly out of a person's bank account. **Credit cards** let people spend money they may not yet have. All these items represent money, even though they don't look like bills. Sometimes, spending money without using cash makes it more difficult to keep track of how much has been spent.

Forms of Cash

Besides bills and coins, many different kinds of objects have been used for money. Some of these examples date back thousands of years. Cultures around the world have used beads, shells, or even cattle as a form of money. Around 500 BC, small pieces of silver were the first coins used.

Cowrie shells were once used for money in Africa.

Modern Minting

Early coins came in many different shapes. Ancient cultures used bars, rings, or lumps of metal. Today, coins are made at government **mints**. Machines cut coins out of strips of metal. An engraver makes a mold for each type of coin so that they are all identical in size and shape and have the correct images on them.

packaging pennies at the United States Mint

Life Cycle of a Dollar Bill

The **United States Bureau of Engraving and Printing** prints approximately 16,650,000 dollar bills each day! The typical life cycle of a $1 bill is a little less than five years. Once the money is printed, it is shipped to the **Federal Reserve Bank**. The Federal Reserve Bank then sends these new bills to different banks. Banks distribute the money to people. Over a short period of time, the bill becomes worn and is returned to the Federal Reserve Bank.

Can you guess why a $50 or a $100 bill has a longer life cycle than a $1 bill?

The Art of Money

Take a close look at a printed bill and you'll find a work of art. First, an artist draws or paints a design for a new bill. Once approved, the design is handed over to a team of engravers. The engravers carve the metal printing plate. It's all done backward so that when the bill is printed, you'll be able to read it.

BUREAU OF ENGRAVING AND PRINTING

Top Secret!

Paper money is 75 percent cotton and 25 percent linen. Colored fibers and special marks are added to discourage **counterfeiters**. Even the recipe for the printing ink is a secret!

Who Prints Money?

A country's money may be printed in another country! Many countries use companies, not government presses, to print paper money. The world's largest banknote printer is De La Rue Currency. The British company prints more than 150 currencies.

Easy Spending

Why would it matter if you spend cash, write a check, or use a debit card? They are all forms of money. Some people find that using cash helps them keep track of how much money is spent. Using a debit card or writing a check is another way to use cash, but both require tracking **expenses**. With cash, when you run out of bills and coins, you are out of money.

The Barter System

In the past, people used a **barter system** instead of money. People exchanged things for what they needed. A hunter might have traded meat for potatoes. A farmer could have offered dairy products in exchange for wheat.

Checking Choices

In the past, people only used cash to buy things. Then, checks and checking accounts became popular. Today, checks aren't used as much. People can quickly pay bills online and spend money using a debit card.

Bills can be paid online using a computer or a phone.

Credit or Debit?

A credit card and a debit card look similar, but they are very different. A debit card is a form of cash, which is money that a person has already earned and stored in the bank. A credit card is used for borrowing money to buy things. Using a credit card means taking out a **loan** from the credit card company. There are **advantages** to using a credit card. People use them for emergencies. They are a safe way to carry money so you don't lose cash. They also help spenders build a **credit history**.

Safe Savings

People used to store their cash at home in piggy banks or under the mattress. Today, it is much more common to have your money deposited in the bank.

Credit History

A credit history explains how much credit a person has and whether he or she usually pays bills on time. A high credit score on a credit report means that a person has a solid financial history. It is easier to borrow money and get more credit with a high credit score. The higher your credit score, the less **interest** you might pay on a loan. That leads to lower monthly loan payments.

Credit Score	500–579	580–619	620–659	660–699	700–759	760–850
Monthly Mortgage Payment ($150,000)	$2,305	$1,917	$1,058	$976	$948	$926
Interest Rate	9.89%	8.91%	7.59%	6.78%	6.49%	6.27%

Overspending

What happens to people who spend money they don't have? Some spenders write checks or use debit cards even when they don't have enough money in the bank. Banks want people to avoid **overdrafts**. So they charge large fees when this happens. Using credit cards can encourage overspending. Credit cards make it quick and easy to buy things. If people continue to have trouble with overspending, it may cause financial problems, or even **bankruptcy** in the years to come.

A Rubber Check

To avoid writing **bounced checks**, smart spenders keep track of what checks have already been written and how much money is in their checking accounts.

After a check is given to a store and sent to the bank, it is scanned and read by a computer. The computer reads the dollar amount and the account number of the check. A computer can sort over 2,400 checks in 1 minute!

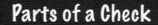

account holder's name   1025

DATE _____ the date the check is written

PAY TO THE ORDER OF ___ recipient of the check _____ $ dollar amount

_____ payment amount _____ DOLLARS 🔒 Security Features Included. Details on Back.

MEMO ___ reminds the account holder how the money is being used ___   the account holder's signature, authorizes the check

⑆000000000⑆ ⑆000000000⑆   ⑈1025

Keeping a record of checks that have been written makes it easier to calculate how much money is in the account.

		TRANSACTION DESCRIPTION	PAYMENT, FEE, WITHDRAWAL (-)	✓	DEPOSIT, CREDIT (+)	BALANCE $	
						5493	00
		COMPANY	$ 15 95			5263	51
		CTRIC BILL	$ 229 99			5150	89
			$ 112 62			5102	39
2362	9/25	GROCERIES	$ 48 50			5066	76
DEBIT	9/27	GAS	$ 35 63			3416	76
DEBIT	9/29	RESTAURANT	$ 1650 00				
2363	10/1	MORTGAGE CO.	$ 4 00			3412	76
DEBIT	10/3	PHARMACY	$ 69 00				
2364	10/5	CABLE	$ 50 00				
2365	10/5	MOBILE PHONE					

15

Creating a Budget

There are so many different ways to spend money, and some are as simple as handing over a plastic card. A **budget** helps spenders keep track of their money. A budget is a record of all the money earned and all the money spent. It tracks income and expenses. It shows spending habits and trends. When a budget is studied closely, a spender can plan for how to best save and spend money.

Charting Your Money

There are many different ways to keep a record of your money. The most basic budgets can be made using pencil and paper. Budgets can also be created using a computer program or website that helps people stay organized.

Budget information can be displayed in line, circle, and bar graphs.

Types of Budgets

A single spender may have a personal budget, while a family might create a household budget. Businesses have budgets. So do cities, states, and countries. Governments keep track of spending and saving money, too.

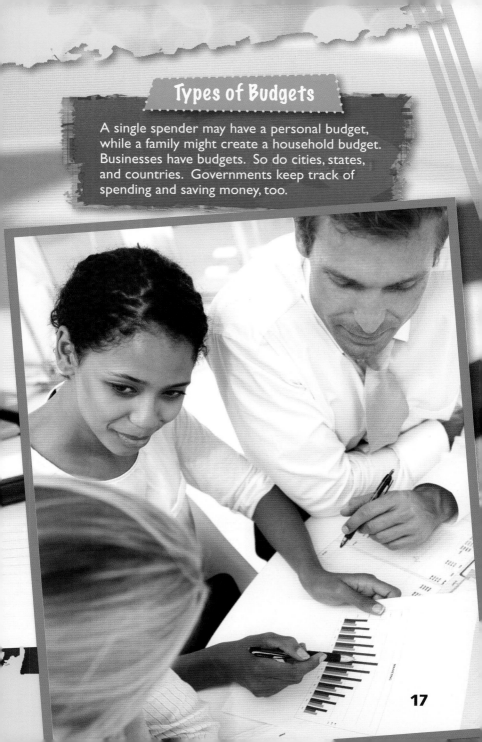

Budget Analysis

Sam, a 16-year-old high school student, created this budget to figure out where his money is going each month. He has a part-time job and is hoping to save money for a car. He wonders why the total amount in his savings account is so low. What do you notice in his budget?

CLOTHES ■ SHOES ■ MOVIES ■ MUSIC
■ VIDEO GAMES ■ FOOD ■ SAVINGS BALANCE

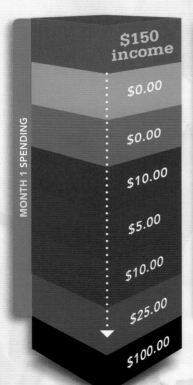

MONTH 1 SPENDING

$150 income

$0.00

$0.00

$10.00

$5.00

$10.00

$25.00

$100.00

MONTH 2 SPENDING

$150 income

$50.00

$50.00

$20.00

$20.00

$10.00

$30.00

$70.00

STOP! THINK...

- How much money has Sam saved in four months?

- Sam works the same amount of hours and earns the same amount of money each month. How does that help him budget his money?

- What could Sam do to save more money?

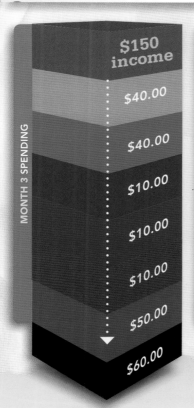

MONTH 3 SPENDING

$150 income

$40.00

$40.00

$10.00

$10.00

$10.00

$50.00

$60.00

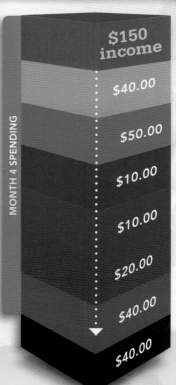

MONTH 4 SPENDING

$150 income

$40.00

$50.00

$10.00

$10.00

$20.00

$40.00

$40.00

Every Penny Counts

Budgets help keep spenders honest. Every single expense, no matter how small, goes in a budget. A budget shows how small purchases can add up to big spending. A $3 smoothie doesn't seem like a lot of money. But if a budget shows that the smoothie is a daily habit, it can mean spending $90 a month for smoothies. If a person bought the ingredients for daily smoothies at a grocery store, it would cost a lot less than $90.

Store Bought versus Homemade

per store-bought smoothie:

$3.50

X 7 days
_____

$24.50 for 7 smoothies

$2.50 juice

+ $1.25 bananas

+ $2.50 blueberries

+ $3.75 peaches
_____

$10 for 7 smoothies

If you receive an allowance at home, the income can be budgeted into three categories: money to spend, money to save, and money to donate to a charity or a cause.

Controlling Your Cash

Take charge of the money you have to spend! Use a chart like this to keep track of where your money goes. By tracking your spending, you'll avoid unpleasant surprises.

What I Bought	Category	Amount
	Food	$20
	Books	$40
	Music	$10
	Clothes	$50
	Total:	**$120**

Feeling Spent

Some people spend their money emotionally. This means they may buy things when they are sad, stressed out, or bored. A budget shows trends in your spending. It might show that you spend money to feel better or forget problems. The act of buying something new makes the spender feel better for a short time. But the feeling won't last.

Pay attention to your moods and spending habits. When are you most likely to buy things you don't need?

Pricey Purchases

There are plenty of big-ticket items for sale and, apparently, plenty of people willing to pay the price.

How about the autograph of William Shakespeare, the world's most famous playwright? His signature is estimated to sell at auction for $5 million. That's fancy penmanship!

Ready to take a dip in the world's most expensive swimming pool? This pool built in Chile is as long as three football fields, holds 66 million gallons of water, and is 115 feet deep! This watery wonder cost a mere $2 billion to build.

At the Westin Hotel in New York, you can order a bagel topped with white truffle cream cheese, goji berries, and leaves of gold. This tasty treat will set you back $1,000!

Where Does the Money Go?

There are lots of ways to spend—and lots of things to buy! People spend money on housing to pay rent or their **mortgage**. They pay for their cars, bus fare, and for other forms of transportation. And they spend a lot on food, buying groceries or eating at restaurants. Education and health care also cost money. People buy clothing, electronics, and household goods. They also like to spend money on entertainment, hobbies, and vacations.

$45.99

$2.99

$60.00

$24.99

> "The person who doesn't know where his next dollar is coming from usually doesn't know where his last dollar went.
>
> —Unknown

A Want or A Need?

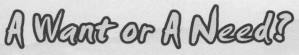

Budgets help people evaluate whether they spend too much money. They also show differences between wants and needs. A *need* is something necessary or essential. It could be a place to live or food to eat. A need is something people must have in order to live a safe and healthy life. A *want* is something that is desired. It is not an essential item. A want includes things that are purchased just for fun, such as extra shoes or movie tickets. One way that people use a budget is to track necessary spending while spending less on wants.

Spend Wisely

If you have extra spending money, consider saving it for a "rainy day." Or buy something you really want after thinking about it for a while and comparing it to other possible purchases.

Cool Coupons

Using coupons is an easy way to save money in your budget. Some coupons give the shopper money back for purchasing another item. Lots of coupons are for things you need to buy anyway. A single coupon might only offer $0.25 off, but using coupons often adds up.

What We Buy

American spending habits change based on what items and activities are popular. If the **economy** is strong, people feel good about spending money.

ENTERTAINMENT
$2,698

5.4%

READING
$118

0.2%

TRANSPORTATION
$8,758

17.6%

The Average American Family

Let's Compare

This pie chart shows the amount the average American household spends in a year. How does your family's spending compare to the average?

HOUSING
$16,920

34.1%

If the economy is weak, then people become nervous about spending. In good economic times, **consumers** might spend more money on vacations and luxury items. In tougher times, people make do with less. Take a look at how the average American family is spending money today.

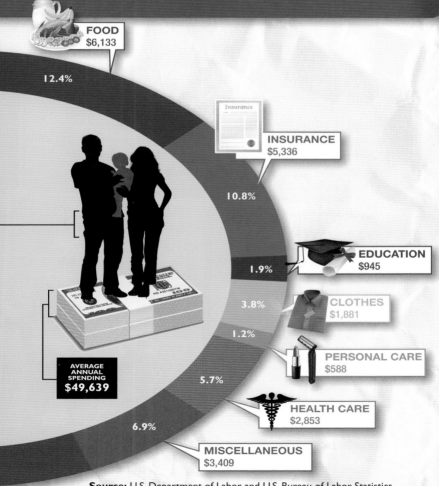

FOOD
$6,133

12.4%

INSURANCE
$5,336

10.8%

EDUCATION
$945

1.9%

CLOTHES
$1,881

3.8%

PERSONAL CARE
$588

1.2%

AVERAGE
ANNUAL
SPENDING
$49,639

5.7%

HEALTH CARE
$2,853

6.9%

MISCELLANEOUS
$3,409

Source: U.S. Department of Labor and U.S. Bureau of Labor Statistics

Analyzing Ads

Stores often advertise their sales. They want to attract as many shoppers as possible. Ads for sales must be appealing to shoppers. They are designed to attract people who are looking for a **bargain**. It is a good idea to always look closely at an advertisement. Sometimes, a store will use sale prices to make it seem as though you are getting a better deal than you are.

Advertising Costs

When you buy an item in a store, your money covers many different expenses. It helps pay for work done by the store employees. It goes toward renting space for the store itself. And it also helps pay for the advertising that may have attracted you to the store in the first place!

STORE COSTS:
PHONES
CLEANING
POWER
COMPUTERS

ADS

WEBSITE

NEWSLETTERS

It All Adds Up

Experts estimate that the average American child watches over 20,000 television commercials in a year, or over 100 a day! One advertising strategy is to create a "nag factor" by showing kids ads that encourage them to buy a product. American children ages 12–17 will ask a parent an average of 9 times for products they have seen on television again and again before parents finally give in.

Need It! Want It!

Advertisers know that feelings influence the decisions we make. So advertisers try to show you how purchasing a certain item will make you feel popular or help you have fun. They use famous people, such as sports heroes or pop stars, to make the product seem great. They show other people having fun with the product. Advertisers use humor to make you laugh and remember what they have to offer.

In 20 minutes, 1,000,000 links are shared on Facebook.

Facts and figures make a product appear more reasonable.

Bright lights used in photography make the product appear as attractive as possible.

Ads use celebrities to make their product more attractive.

OWN THE ROAD, BUY A ROADSTER.

This ad is designed to make you wonder, "Am I cool enough to own this car?"

Special Spending

There are times in life that people must spend a lot of money on a special expense. It may be temporary. Someone may need a new car to replace an old one that broke down. Or money may be needed to purchase a home. A couple may need to spend a lot of money when they get married. College **tuition** is also a special expense. Going to college is an important goal for many young people, but college costs a lot. Paying for college requires planning.

College Loans

To pay for college, students may take out a loan. A bank will give them money to pay for college, but they must pay it back after they graduate. Some organizations give out **scholarships** for exceptional students. This money must be used for college tuition but doesn't need to be paid back.

Stay in School!

The more education you have, the higher your income is likely to be. Those who earn professional degrees are often in the highest income brackets. Those who make it through only some of high school tend to make the least amount of money. How long do you plan to go to school?

Average Salaries
(Based on the 2010 U.S. Census)

Professional Degree (doctor, lawyer)	$127,803
Doctoral Degree	$103,054
Master's Degree	$73,738
Bachelor's Degree	$56,665
Associate's Degree	$32,295
High School Graduate	$30,627
Some High School Education	$20,241

College can be more affordable if you start at a community college or work during the summer.

35

Strange Sales

People buy and sell some very odd and interesting items. Sometimes, there's no telling what value an item may have and how much someone is willing to pay for it.

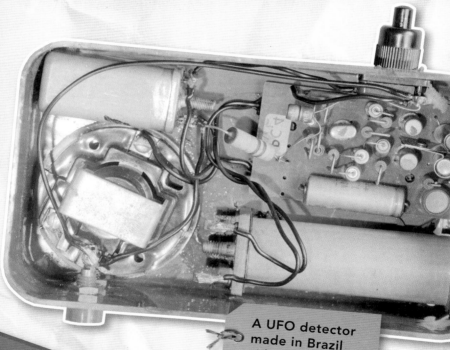

A UFO detector made in Brazil sold for $135.03.

A piece of gum chewed by singer Britney Spears sold for $14,000.

Someone purchased a cornflake in the shape of Illinois for $1,350.

This woman had an ad tattooed on her forehead for $10,000.

Big Bucks

Many people complain that a dollar doesn't go as far as it used to. There is some truth to that statement. What we can buy with a dollar today is not what people bought for a dollar 10, 20, or 50 years ago. What does a penny buy today? Not much! You might find a piece of candy for one cent. A hundred years ago, you could have spent a few pennies to buy a gallon of milk. What does a billion dollars buy you today? A whole lot! Most people will never even see the kinds of luxury items that billionaires buy.

The Cost of Inflation

Inflation is the gradual rise in the prices of goods and services over time. Things cost more today than they did years ago. This means that the money you have today is worth less than the same amount of money was worth in the past.

It actually costs more than one cent to make a penny! That means a penny costs more to make than it is worth to spend.

$6.69 $6.69 $6.69 $6.69 $6.69 $6.69

Big Spender

What can you buy with your dollar? It depends on how many you have! Take a look at the items below to see how much you can buy for one dollar or one billion dollars.

$1,000,000,000
tropical island

$1,000,000
luxurious house

$100,000
recreational
vehicle

$10,000
compact car

$1
100 paper clips

$10
Frisbee

$100
skateboard

$1,000
diamond earrings

Money Around the World

The spending habits of people around the world vary by country. People are limited by the size of their income. A country's economy is an important factor as well. Money doesn't go as far in countries with high inflation rates. It costs more to buy goods and services in these countries. People are also influenced by what other people buy. In some countries, people prefer to spend their money on recreation rather than on clothing, for example.

Exchange Rates

Many countries use their own types of bills and coins, but all these bills and coins are not worth the same. The **exchange rate** is the rate at which one **currency** is traded for another. This rate is constantly changing. A dollar in the United States is worth different amounts depending on when and where it is exchanged.

Spending Around the World

Check out the percentage of income the average citizen spends each month in some common categories.

China

Housing = 8%
Food = 19%
Entertainment = 7%
Autos = 3%
Health care = 6%
Education = 7%

India

Housing = 14%
Food = 23%
Entertainment = 3%
Autos = 5%
Health care = 6%
Education = 17%

Russia

Housing = 12%
Food = 34%
Entertainment = 6%
Autos = 5%
Health care = 5%
Education = 3%

United States

Housing = 34%
Food = 12%
Entertainment = 5%
Autos = 17%
Health care = 6%
Education = 2%

Source: Credit Suisse Emerging Consumer Survey

DIG DEEPER!

Money Mind Reader

Take the following quiz to learn how you see money.

1 When you receive your weekly allowance, you think:

A. I know that somehow it will be gone by the end of the week.
B. I'll save this now and consider how to spend it later.
C. I can't wait to hit the shopping mall to see what I can buy.
D. I'm going to put this in my savings account right away.

2 When you want something expensive, you think:

A. I'm going to buy it now even though I can't afford it.
B. If I carefully watch my budget and save over time, I'll be able to buy this later.
C. Even though I don't have enough money, someone will lend me money to buy it.
D. There's no way I would ever pay that much for this item even though I like it a lot.

3 When you are feeling down, you think:

A. There is nothing I can buy that will cheer me up.

B. Brainstorming ways to save money will make me feel better.

C. As soon as I can get to the store to buy something, I'll feel great.

D. If I focus on saving money, then I might feel better.

4 When someone gives you money as a present, you think:

A. I wonder what I can do with this cash.

B. I'm going to save a portion. The rest I'll spend on something I've been wanting for a while.

C. I won't be hanging on to these bucks for long.

D. My bank account is going to grow some more today.

Take a closer look at your answers.

If you picked mostly **A**s, you don't think too much about money. You're carefree about cash.

If you selected mostly **B**s, you enjoy thinking about saving and spending. You're thoughtful about money.

If you chose mostly **C**s, you make use of your cash right away. You're a big spender.

If you answered mostly **D**s, you like to save every cent. You're ultra thrifty.

Making Money Matter

Having money and using it wisely can definitely make your life more comfortable. But do you know that the money you earn can also help others? When you earn money, you can improve lives around the world. So how can you make the most of your money?

Something for Everyone

There are many different kinds of **charities**. Most will accept any size donation you are able to make. You can choose from charities for poor children, homeless animals, or polluted waters. There are also charitable organizations that focus on finding cures for diseases, saving endangered species, and promoting the arts.

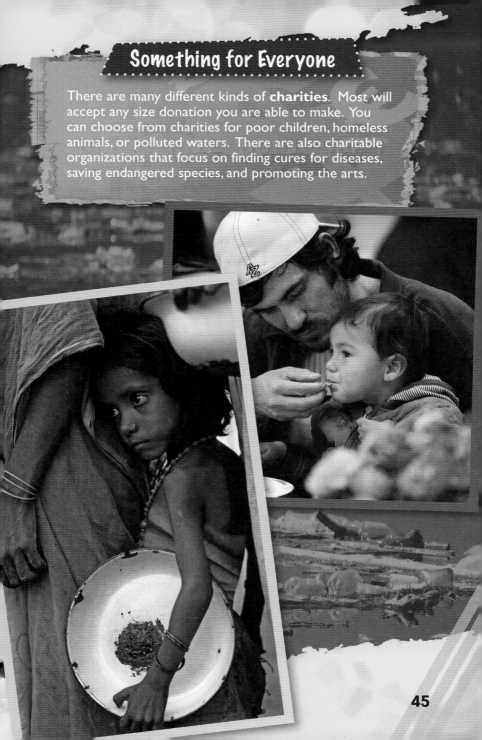

Tax Time

People may choose to spend money on items and services that they want or need. These are part of a budget. Adults are also required to pay **taxes**. A tax is a fee the government collects to pay for services. Taxes are paid to city, state, and federal governments. They are used to keep our towns, cities, and country in good condition. They also provide services that all people use and share. For example, taxes help support public schools and roads. They also help pay for garbage collection and police and fire departments. Most people agree that everyone should pay their fair share to keep these services going.

War and Taxes

Many taxes began in wartime. Great Britain created an **income tax** in 1799 to raise money for the Napoleonic Wars. Germany started a **sales tax** during World War I. These governments planned to collect the taxes for a short time. But after the wars ended, they continued the taxes. Other countries started using the same taxes.

INTERNAL REVENUE SERVICE

The Big Day

The **Internal Revenue Service (IRS)** is in charge of collecting taxes in the United States. April 15 is usually the day that tax paperwork is due unless it falls on a weekend or holiday.

Check with a CPA

Many people take their tax forms to a **Certified Public Accountant (CPA)**. The CPA knows the most recent laws and how to fill out the forms accurately.

Types of Taxes

Workers pay taxes on the money they make. Income tax is the amount of taxes workers pay based on the amount of money they make. In many places, sales taxes are collected on items that shoppers buy. Each state decides how much the sales-tax rate should be. Sales tax is usually around 4 to 9 percent of the cost of the item purchased.

Are Taxes Fair?

The subject of taxes can be a tricky one to talk about with others. People have a lot of different opinions about the taxes others should pay. Is it fair if we all pay the same amount of income tax? Or does it make more sense for wealthier people to pay higher taxes?

If you buy a shirt for $20, then a 5 percent sales tax would add $1 to the cost of the shirt. What would you pay with a 9 percent sales tax?

Taxes Around the World

Income tax rates vary by country. Many countries have a **progressive tax**, which means that the tax rate is higher for those earning more income. Check out these rates for countries around the world. Each country has a progressive tax. The rates below are the maximum rate any taxpayer must pay.

Bulgaria
10%

Egypt
20%

United States
35%

Ireland
48%

Finland
49%

Aruba
59%

Source: KPMG Individual Income Tax Rates Table for 2012

Giving It Away

Sometimes, there is extra room in a budget. Of course, the extra cash can be spent or saved. But there is one more option for that money. It can be donated to a good cause. Donating money feels good. People can choose the kind of organizations that they support. Many groups rely on **philanthropy** to pay for programs and services for people in need. Many families struggle with paying for things they need, like food or shelter. When others who have more can share resources, it makes life easier for people in need. When people donate money to a favorite charity, the government does not tax this money. The taxpayer gets to pay fewer taxes and also contribute to the local or global community.

Close to Home

Some people like to give money to their church or religious institution. The money pays for things needed within the religious community.

PLEASE CONTRIBUTE TO OUR
TSUNAMI
RELIEF
FUND

Drop your contributions into "PhilBert" in Center Court. We will deliver them to the American Friends Service Committee.

Thank You

Churches may raise funds for disaster victims.

Personal Connections

People often decide to donate to a good cause because of a personal experience. If a loved one has cancer, donating to a group that does research in search of a cure for cancer can have real personal meaning.

This woman wears a pink ribbon to show she supports the fight against cancer.

Pass It On

You don't need a lot of extra money to be able to make a donation. Some people start by saving small amounts over time. Then, those small amounts grow into larger donations. Even something as simple as a bake sale can raise enough money to make a difference. Getting sponsors and walking or running in a race is another way to raise money.

Celebrities Give Back

Many famous wealthy people find ways to give back to communities in need. For example, many major league sports teams work in their own communities, helping and inspiring young students who are facing hard times along with their families.

Professional basketball player Vladimir Radmanovic reads to students.

Dividing Up Donations

The Bill & Melinda Gates foundation spends millions of dollars each year on a wide range of charities. They support research for new vaccines to save children around the world from deadly illnesses. They also partner with organizations to support fine teachers and good schools so that all children in the United States will receive an excellent education.

Businessman and philanthropist Bill Gates admires the work of these science students.

DIG DEEPER!

A Little Goes a Long Way

Charities appreciate any donation no matter how small. In fact, just a small amount of money can have a huge impact, especially if everyone gives a little bit. From the cost of a pack of gum to the price of a nice dinner, see how far a donation can go toward helping others.

Purchase a grove of trees in Zambia. These trees make soil rich enough to grow important crops.

Buy blankets and bibs for babies in need.

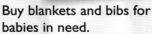

Pay for a child's vaccine against polio.

Pay for the education of a student in Sri Lanka.

Money Matters

How you manage your money can play a big part in your life. You decide what you will buy. You determine how much you will save. You can also choose to give back to charities and make a difference to people. Planning what you do with the money you have and the money you earn can be tricky, but it can also be a lot of fun. And every decision you make adds up!

Glossary

advantages—benefits

allowance—money given to a child so that he or she can learn about saving and spending money

bankruptcy—a legal status that happens when a person or a group cannot pay money that is owed

bargain—a good deal or sale price

barter system—a system of trading goods or services that does not involve money

bounced checks—checks written without money to pay for them

budget—a plan for saving and spending money

Certified Public Accountant (CPA)—an accountant who has passed certain exams and met all other laws and licensing requirements to be certified by a state

charities—organizations focused on helping others

checks—written statements that authorize money to be withdrawn from a person's account

consumers—people who spend money on goods and services

counterfeiters—people who make illegal copies, often of money

credit cards—cards that allow shoppers to buy things using borrowed money and pay for them later

credit history—a person's financial record, used by banks to determine whether someone qualifies for loans and other services

currency—anything that is widely accepted as money

debit cards—cards that automatically deduct cash from a shopper's account when he or she buys something

economy—the process or system by which goods or services are produced, sold, and bought in a country

exchange rate—the rate at which one currency is traded for another

expenses—money spent to create products or services

Federal Reserve Bank—the bank that supervises and controls the flow of money in American banks

income—money received or earned

income tax—a tax on the money a person earns

inflation—a general increase in prices

interest—the money a bank or organization pays a person for investing in them

Internal Revenue Service (IRS)—the United States government agency in charge of collecting taxes and enforcing tax laws

loan—an amount of borrowed money, often given with the promise that interest will be repaid

mints—where coins are made

mortgage—a loan for a house

overdrafts—situations in which money is taken from a bank account and the leftover balance goes below zero when there isn't enough money to cover the purchase

philanthropy—a spirit of goodwill toward all people, especially when expressed in active and generous efforts to help others

progressive tax—a tax rate that increases so people earning more money pay higher taxes

sales tax—tax placed on the sale of certain items

scholarships—financial help for students that does not need to be repaid

taxes—fees paid to the government to support local or national services

tuition—a fee charged for taking classes at a school or a university

United States Bureau of Engraving and Printing—where American paper money is printed

!ndex

advertisement, 30

Africa, 6

allowance, 4, 20, 42

Aruba, 49

bankruptcy, 14

bargain, 30

barter system, 10

Bill & Melinda Gates foundation, 53

bounced checks, 14

Brazil, 36

budget, 16–19, 20, 22, 26–27, 42, 46, 50

cash, 6, 10–12, 43, 50

Certified Public Accountant (CPA), 47

charities, 45, 53–54, 56

checks, 6, 11, 14–15

Chile, 23

China, 41, 55

college, 34–35

commercials, 31

consumers, 29

counterfeiters, 9

coupons, 27

credit cards, 6, 12, 14

credit history, 12–13

currency, 40

De La Rue Currency, 9

debit cards, 6, 10–12, 14

economy, 28–29, 40

education, 24, 35, 41, 53, 55

Egypt, 49

engraver, 7–8

exchange rate, 40

expenses, 10, 16, 20, 30, 34

Federal Reserve Bank, 8

Finland, 49

Gates, Bill, 53

Illinois, 37

income, 4, 16, 18–20, 35, 40–41, 48–49

income tax, 46, 48–49

inflation, 38, 40

Internal Revenue Service (IRS), 47

Ireland, 49

Mauritania, 55

mints, 7

New York, 23

overdrafts, 14

overspending, 14

philanthropy, 50

piggy banks, 12

progressive tax, 49

Radmanovic, Vladimir, 52

sales tax, 46, 48

scholarships, 34

Shakespeare, William, 23

Spears, Britney, 37

Sri Lanka, 55

taxes, 46–50

tuition, 34

United States, 7, 40–41, 47, 49, 53

United States Bureau of Engraving and Printing, 8

Zambia, 54

Bibliography

Chatzky, Jean. *Not Your Parents' Money Book: Making, Saving, and Spending Your Own Money.* **Simon & Schuster Books for Young Readers, 2010.**

In this book, a financial expert makes understanding money—from how it's made to how you spend it—easy. Learn how to get rid of bad spending habits and make smart financial choices. The author answers questions about money from real kids just like you.

Cribb, Joe. *Money.* **DK Publishing, 2005.**

Explore the history of money around the world as well as today's international currency. See what the earliest coins looked like, how money is made, and how to detect fake money.

Hall, Alvin. *Show Me The Money.* **DK Publishing, 2008.**

Learn the basics about income expenses, economics, business, and how money works around the world. Color photos, games, and cartoons make learning about money matters fun.

Linecker, Adelia Cellini. *What Color is Your Piggy Bank? Entrepreneurial Ideas for Self-Starting Kids.* **Lobster Press, 2004.**

Learn how to make money doing what you love right now. Quizzes, links to templates, and profiles of real young business owners will jump start you on your own road to success.

Reichblum, Charles. *What Happens to a Torn Dollar Bill?* **Black Dog & Leventhal Publishers, 2006.**

Discover bizarre and fascinating facts about money. In this book, Dr. Knowledge covers everything about money from why there is a pyramid on the dollar bill and who invented the credit card to why money is called *money* and who was the youngest person to become a millionaire.

More to Explore

Design Your Own Bill

http://www.newmoney.gov/newmoney/dyob/index.html

Make your own custom dollar bill. You decide the value, border, images, and color of your bill with just a few clicks of a mouse. When you are done, you can print your bill or e-mail it to a friend.

EconEdLink

http://www.econedlink.org

This website about personal finance is designed for both teachers and students. Click on the *student* link and look for fun learning activities and games about money management and banking.

Hands on Banking

http://www.handsonbanking.org/en/

Take charge of your finances and future with this website. Just click on the *Kids* link and follow the alien Zing on an interactive adventure to learn about you and your money, budgeting, savings, checking, and credit.

Money and Stuff

http://www.moneyandstuff.info

Here, you'll find worksheets to create your own budget, arcade games, videos, and other fun money activities.

Planet Orange

http://www.orangekids.com

Through your travels on Planet Orange, you will discover how to best handle your money. You will find games and activities to teach you about earning, spending, saving, and investing.

About the Author

Christine Dugan earned her B.A. from the University of California, San Diego. She taught elementary school for several years before taking on a different challenge in the field of education. She has worked as a product developer, a writer, an editor, and a sales assistant for various educational publishing companies. In recent years, Christine earned her M.A. in education and is currently working as a freelance author and editor. She lives in the Pacific Northwest, where she happily spends and saves money with her husband and two daughters.